THE WAY OF CONSCIOUS LIVING

LOIS TSCHIDA
&
GERMAINE SMITH

THE CENTER FOR HEALING PRESS

© 2017 by Lois Tschida and Germaine Smith.
All rights reserved.

Photographs by Lois Tschida.
Prose by Germaine Smith.

ISBN : 978-0-9960421-3-0 (print)
Library of Congress Control Number: 2017911707

All rights reserved.
No portion of this publication may be reproduced or transmitted in any form or by any means, electronic or mechanical, including photocopying, recording, or capturing on any information storage and retrieval system, without permission in writing from the publisher, except by a reviewer who may quote brief passages in a critical article or review to be printed in a magazine or newspaper, or electronically transmitted on radio, television, or Internet.

For photograph reprint or sale information, contact Lois at:
         ldtschida@hotmail.com or www.sharedspiritcards.com
For book reprint permission, email germ@thecenterforhealing.us.

The Center for Healing Press is the imprint of The Center for Healing.
Contact: germ@thecenterforhealing.us.

 Front Cover Picture ©: St. John's Abbey and University, Collegeville, MN
Back Cover Picture ©. Minnehaha Creek, Minneapolis, MN.
All rights reserved.

DEDICATION

To my husband
Bob Tschida
who has been a Constant Beacon on my Journey
"Go Easy"

DEDICATION

To my steadfast companions on the way:
Roger Bernstrom
Anthony Bosca

THANKS TO
Connor Blacksher
Mary McPherson

TABLE OF CONTENTS

0.	Introduction to Conscious Living	6
1.	The Way of Facing Fear 　　Minnehaha Park 　　Minneapolis, MN	12
2.	The Way of Investigating Suffering 　　Lake Street & Ford Parkway Bridges 　　Minneapolis, MN	18
3.	The Way of Releasing Pain 　　Minnehaha Falls 　　Minneapolis, MN	28
4.	The Way to Re-Membering God 　　St. John's Abbey & University 　　Collegeville, MN	36
5.	The Way of Healing Wounds 　　Fort Snelling State Park 　　St. Paul, MN	48
6.	The Way of Recovering Sanity 　　Lake Phalen 　　St. Paul, MN	58
7.	The Way of Understanding One 　　Lake Harriet Minneapolis, MN	66
8.	The Way of Experiencing Joy 　　Walker's Choice	

0.

INTRODUCTION
TO
THE WAY
OF
CONSCIOUS LIVING

St. John's Abbey & University
Collegeville, MN

The Way of Conscious Living is a series of meditative walks,
    opportunities to pause for a few hours out in nature,
    designed to integrate body, heart, mind, and soul.
One walks a specific route, stopping for reflection and meditation
    as a means to healing from denial and escapism
    in order to embrace conscious living.

HISTORY

I got the idea after learning about the Camino de Santiago
    or the Way of St. James in Spain.
In ancient times, Celtic/Iberian tribes traveled by foot
    to reach the coast of Spain.
This was both a physical and a spiritual endeavor:
    crossing long distances over often difficult terrain
    in search of a change in one's life.
The objective was to reach the coast;
    to watch the sun set into the great expanse of water
    that is the Atlantic Ocean.

People came from many directions
    with one destination as their goal:
        today's Cape Finisterre.
The Romans would call it "Fenestrae",
    literally "the end of the world" in Latin.
Upon arriving, the ancient pagans would bury their clothes
    to symbolize the end of something old,
    the beginning of something new.

By the ninth century, Christians were using the roads
    as pilgrimage routes to the tomb of St. James.
While the destination has changed from Cape Finisterre
    to the Cathedral of Santiago,
    the reasons for the walk remain.
Some go with hopes of a new life; some go as a penance;
    some go yearning for spiritual awakening.
I loved the concept of "The Way"

but did not want to go to Spain.
So I wrote this as a means to utilize the objectives
in a modern fashion.

GUIDELINES

1. Walk "The Way".
Do not run, bike, rollerblade.
The point is to be with yourself
to slow down and have time to feel and listen.
This is not about speed
but about being present to your body, heart, mind, soul.

If you don't live near the geographical sites I chose,
choose one of your own.
If you have limited mobility,
do the "The Way" in your house or around your block.
If you are immobile, do "The Way" in your imagination.

2. Walk "The Way" in solitude.
That means by yourself.
Turn off the phone, the tunes, the Web
so that this is time for you.
Alone.

3. Safety first.
At all times, the safety of yourself and others is most imperative.

4. Healing is the goal.
"The Way" is not meant as penance or mortification.
Bring what you need
such as drinking water, sunscreen,
proper clothing, good shoes, etc.

5. Flexibility is wonderful.
Follow the layout. Or not.
If you try to follow the layout but get lost or take a different trail

      welcome it as an adventure.
If you are a nonconformist, create your own route.
Wherever works for you.
6. Appreciate the process.
Leave perfectionism at the recycle bin
      to be transformed into appreciation.
Celebrate the unfolding of the process and
      trust that unfolding will bring what you need.

7. Any order is good.
There are seven options;
      each stand independently.
Listen to your soul and begin.

1.

THE WAY OF FACING FEAR

Minnehaha Creek
Minneapolis, MN

LOCATION   Minnehaha Falls Park, Minneapolis, MN
BRING   Drinking water, feather, small stone
LENGTH   2 miles
TIME   2 hours

MEDITATION A
[Arrive at Minnehaha Park.]

This ritual is centered on facing fear.
It's goal is to master the turning point of confronting terror
	and not escaping into denial
	or medicating oneself in addiction.
It is a turning point of facing fear
	and embracing consciousness.
Fear is not to be conquered, as if it were an enemy in a battle.
That would only perpetuate and increase the fear.
Fear is to be admitted, faced, owned, in order to be healed.
As I walk to the Falls,
	with each step I set my intention of facing my fear.

MEDITATION B
[Walk to the bridge over the Falls.]
May I be open—open to admitting I am afraid
	open to seeing fear not as an enemy to be escaped
	but a visitor bearing insights
	open to facing fear so that it will no longer possess me
		but that I may possess myself.
As I walk to the corner of Minnehaha Parkway
	and 46th Avenue South,
	with each step may I breathe in courage.

MEDITATION C
[Walk to the sidewalk along Minnehaha Parkway.
Turn right, walk east along Minnehaha Parkway
	to the corner of 46th Avenue South.]

"Fear keeps us focused on the past or worried about the future.
If we can acknowledge our fear, we can realize that right now
	we are okay.
Right now, today, we are still alive

and our bodies are working marvelously.
Our eyes can still see the beautiful sky.
Our ears can still hear the voices of our loved ones."[1]

I used to think that fear motivated me to be prepared for anything.
Now I realize it just paralyzes me in despair.

[Take out the stone and hold it.]
As I walk to the middle of the bridge over the Mississippi River
    with each step may I breathe in hope.

MEDITATION D
[Walk one block north on 46th Avenue South.
Cross 46th Street East.
Turn right onto the Ford Parkway Bridge.
Walk halfway across the Bridge.]

"You gain strength, courage and confidence
    by every experience in which you really stop
    to look fear in the face.
You are able to say to yourself,
    'I have lived through this horror.
I can take the next thing that comes along.'
You must do the thing you think you cannot do."[2]

From the fear of anger,
    grant me serenity to face what I do not like or want.
From the fear of pain,
    grant me acceptance to let go of all I no longer possess.
From the fear of loss,
    grant me understanding to remember that nothing
    ever dies, only changes.
From the fear of loneliness,
    grant me serenity that You are always with me.
From the fear of insecurity,
    grant that I live in the trust
    that all is unfolding as it should.

---

1   Thich Nhat Hanh, http://www.brainyquote.com/ quotes/authors/t/thich_nhat_hanh.html (February, 4, 2016).

2   Eleanor Roosevelt, http://www.brainyquote.com/quotes/ authors/e/eleanor_roosevelt.html (February, 4, 2016).

MEDITATION E
[Continue across the Mississippi River.
Safely cross to the south side of the Ford Parkway Bridge.
Walk halfway back across the Bridge.]

"What is needed, rather than running away or controlling
    or suppressing or any other resistance,
    is understanding fear;
    that means: watch it, learn about it,
    come directly into contact with it.
We are to learn about fear, not how to escape from it."[3]

O Spirit of all creation,
May this stone be a symbol of my fear, an image of my inability
    to move forward toward wholeness.
May I open every cell of my being to facing my fear to be open to
    owning it so I may learn from it, and then heal it.
As I drop this stone into the Mississippi
    and it sinks to the river bottom,
    may it become the bedrock and foundation
    upon which I create my authentic and highest self.

[When it is safe for all on the river release the stone into the river.
Set your intention on releasing fear
    letting it sink like the stone into the river bottom.
Take the feather & hold it.]

As I walk to the Falls Pavilion, may I breathe in liberation.

MEDITATION F
Walk to 46th Avenue South, turn left.
Walk to Minnehaha Parkway, turn right.
Walk to the Falls Pavilion]
"It is not the critic who counts;
    not the one who points out how the strong man stumbles,
    or where the doer of deeds could have done them better.
The credit belongs to the one who is actually in the arena,
    whose face is marred by dust and sweat and blood;
    who strives valiantly; who errs,
    who comes up short again and again,
    because there is no effort without error and shortcoming;
    but who does actually strive to do the deeds;
    who knows great enthusiasms,
    who spends himself in a worthy cause;
    who knows in the end the triumph of high achievement,

---

[3]   Jiddu Krishnamurti, http://www.brainyquote.com/quotes/authors/j/jiddu_krishnamurti.html (February, 4, 2016).

and if he fails, at least fails while daring greatly,
so that his place shall never be with
those cold and timid souls
who neither know victory nor defeat."[4]

O Higher Power, grant me courage to step
    into the arena with my fear
    to err and get back up again and again.
O Spirit of Integrity, grant me wisdom to know worthy causes
    especially the most worthy of causes: my highest good.
O Divine Master, grant me the integrity to understand
    that who I am afraid of—
    is me.

MEDITATION G
[Walk to the Falls & down the ramp.
Walk along the south side of Minnehaha Creek
    before the Creek gets to the Falls.]

Feathers symbolize that one is on the right path.
Today, I am not receiving feathers but releasing feathers
    to symbolize that despite my fears.
I willing surrender to the will of the Spirit of all creation.

Spirit of all creation, I turn my will and life over to you.
As I drop this feather into the waters
    may it symbolize my willingness
    to allow You to set my course.

I commit to facing my fears and embrace the path You set for me.
As You move this feather through wind and current,
    I commit to facing fear and learning its lessons.
As this feather disappears from my sight,
    I commit to trusting in Your Presence
    as I walk my path to my greatest self and my highest good
    to heal myself and the six generations before me .

[When ready, release the feather into the Minnehaha Creek.]

Whenever my fear arises, may I remember
    I have the power to release it.
    I have the courage to learn pains' difficult lessons
    trusting that my Higher Power is setting my course.
So be it. Amen.

[4]   Theodore Roosevelt, http://www.brainyquote.com/quotes/_authors/t/theodore_roosevelt.html (February, 4, 2016).

2.

THE WAY
OF
INVESTIGATING SUFFERING

Ford Parkway Bridge
Minneapolis, MN

LOCATION   Lake Street & Ford Parkway Bridges, Minneapolis
BRING   Drinking water
LENGTH   3 miles
TIME   2 hours

MEDITATION A
[Arrive at West River Road near Ford Parkway Bridge.]

This ritual focuses uncovering the sufferings we carry—
    sufferings we are aware of and sufferings we have buried
    deeply in hopes that they would never surface again.

Investigating suffering is vital.
When I choose ignorance or denial
    suffering festers underneath my skin, my heart, my spirit.
I remain unconscious and stuck.

Suffering is a human state for all people.
    painful yet purposeful
    heavy yet illuminating
    scarring yet restoring
    temporary if I am willing to enter its depths
        and feel its fury.

I suffer.
To heal my injuries, I first must be aware
    of the deep and secret places where I ache.

MEDITATION B
[Walk the West River Road walking trail to 42nd Street]
I suffer with the pain of abandonment.

Harsh words, harsher actions have scarred me.
Abuse, neglect, have left me isolated and lonely.
My childhood knows the depths of suffering
    when abandoned by tenderness.
My adulthood knows the depths of suffering
    from abandonment of self-love.
I have been deserted by everyone, including God.

Where are you, O Divine One?
Why do I feel You have left me, desolated and apart?

Abandonment pierces my very being,
        leaving me feeling so unlovable and unwanted.
I long to be re-connected, re-joined.
I ache to feel I belong to humanity,
        to my self,
        to You.

MEDITATION C
[Walk the West River Road walking trail to 38th Street]

I suffer with the knowledge of failure.

I have made so many grievous mistakes and errors:
        times I screwed up what I needed to do
        times I refused to do what was asked of me.

My failures seem unescapable:
        some of them I can do nothing about
        most I have no idea how to rectify.

Failure weighs me down into the pit of worthlessness
        an ugly prison of self-hate with no parole date.

MEDITATION D
[Continue to 36th Street]

I suffer in the depths of despair.

Despair has many names that all speak of the same black hole:
        depression that encases me in thick fog of inertia
        hopelessness that sucks me down like quicksand
        desolation that chokes off any confidence or optimism.

I am lost—with no way out.

MEDITATION E
[Continue to 34th Street]

I suffer from heartache.

I am so alone.
Few friends grace my door; my heart beaks.
Some have just walked out; some have faded into the distance.
I ache without community.

My career path seems closed; my heart breaks.
I stepped off the cliff of security and left my secure job behind.
I know it was the right path but I am still in free-fall—
        no ground beneath me, no safety net I can see.
I ache to be invested in a career that fuels my passion.

My family doesn't know who I am; my heart breaks.
I often feel like I am on the outside looking in.
I ache to be seen and known.

MEDITATION F
[Walk to the bottom of the ramp leading up to Lake Street]

I suffer from grief.

I grieve that my body does not work as I want it to,
        as well as it used to.
Every day, my knees are stiff, my back hurts.
        Why is my body failing me?
        Why will it not heal itself like it used to?

I grieve my eye sight continues to fail.
The loss of sight, of driving privileges,
        of my ability to read terrifies me.
        How will I get around?
        How will I earn a living?

I grieve that my addictions persist: my weight yo-yos.
        Why can't I be like others?
        Why am I so powerless?

I grieve that family and friends have died.
I know this is the unfolding of the cycle of life and death
> but I still miss them.
> How do I fill the hole left by their deaths?
> How do I go on without them?

MEDITATION G
[Walk halfway across the Lake Street Bridge.
Face south, watch the river flow away]

As I look down at the Mississippi River,
> I stand willing to let my suffering flow into the water
> and be carried downstream into the ocean of healing.
Discharging suffering brings great freedom and space.
> What will take its place?

Suffering is purposeful illuminating and restorative—
> when its gifts are embraced.
Though difficult to think of suffering as having gifts, it does.
It offers: trust, forgiveness, hope, acceptance, and faith.
May I be open to filling the space left
> by investigating and owning my suffering
> with the gifts and lessons it offers.

MEDITATION H
[Walk across Lake Street Bridge.
Take ramp down to the East River Road walking trail.]

The suffering of abandonment is healed by trust.
Though I do not always feel your presence,
> You have held my hand through it all.
Every step, you were there.
When I was stuck, you stood beside me.
When I was ready, you illuminated my next step.

Teach me the depths of trust
> to acknowledge my fear of abandonment
>> so I will find you present
> to know without question that You have been
>> and already are with me.

MEDITATION I
[Walk the East River Road walking trail to Summit Avenue.]
The suffering from failure is healed by forgiveness
    and making amends.
Teach me to forgive myself for all my mistakes and errors
    all the things I did intentionally
    and unintentionally
    that hurt others or myself.

Teach me to forgive myself for being human
    when I wanted to be perfect
    for wallowing in victimhood that fueled my self-destruction
    for rejecting my authenticity in favor of
    superficial conformity
    for being serious when I needed to play
    for hating myself when I wanted to be loved.

Give me the courage to make amends to all I have injured
    starting with myself.
Help me to make a list of all whom I have harmed
    seeking not my comfort but a clean slate.

MEDITATION J
[Walk the East River Road walking trail to Princeton Avenue]
The suffering from despair is healed by hope.

Teach me to breathe deep the oxygen of hope.
No matter what my circumstance,
    there are always many who suffer more than I.
No matter how much despair tries to drag me down,
    I have successes to celebrate.

MEDITATION K
[Continue to Jefferson Avenue]

The suffering from heartache is healed by acceptance.

The lesson from heartache is a difficult one
    because it demands I accept what is offered
    without denial, judgement or complaint.
Acceptance is really letting go of the many things I can't control.
Teach me to be open
    to what gifts others share with me with gratitude.
As friends and family come and go
    bringing and sharing their gifts
        may I be accepting and grateful for however long
            they are in my life.

I surrender my career and life to you and recognize
    that I am right where I need to be.
Teach me to accept that whatever path I am on
    it holds the lessons I need right now.
Help me to face those lessons with dignity and patience.

MEDITATION L
[Continue to Randolph Avenue.]

The suffering from grief is healed by faith.

Teach me to increase my faith in You, O Divine One,
    that I follow You more willingly.
Increase my faith that You are guiding my path—
    I am not in charge of my life.

Give me the courage to surrender, knowing You are present.
Increase my faith that You will be made clearer
    through my loss of vision.
Give me courage to surrender
    as my body's efficacy diminishes and death nears.
Increase my faith in You when death takes my friends and family.
Give me the courage to surrender;
    knowing they have fulfilled their journey
    and are going home.

MEDITATION M
[Walk to middle of the Ford Parkway Bridge]

Investigating suffering is vital.
I wish to live in freedom from suffering's drag
        to be an active participant in life's upholding
        rather than a cooperating victim.

I choose to face my suffering
        and that choice rewards me with the gifts of
        trust, forgiveness, hope, acceptance, and faith.
With these, suffering has no hold.
With these, I am restored
        every breath becomes refreshment
        happiness becomes reality.

MEDITATION N
[Walk to starting point]

Grant me courage, O Divine One,
        to face my sufferings as they arrive.
I choose to investigate suffering.
From this point on, may I be fearless and grateful
        for every lesson and gift that suffering offers to me.

3.
THE WAY OF RELEASING PAIN

Minnehaha Falls
Minneapolis, MN

LOCATION	Minnehaha Falls, Minneapolis, MN
BRING	Drinking water, small bag for garbage bag salted-in-the-shell sunflower seeds, list of my pains/sufferings on small paper
LENGTH	1 mile, 113 steps
TIME	1 hour

MEDITATION A
[Arrive at Minnehaha Park.]

This ritual focuses on embracing my pain in order to release it
    so I can heal my woundedness
      and move forward in my life.
We are all wounded
    suffering from losses that at times paralyze us.
Whatever my pain is,
    [grief because of death, loss of a relationship,
    job insecurity, abuse, physical disease,
    conflict without resolution, mental illness, addiction,
    spiritual suffering, the absence of hope, etc.]
    my pain can be soothed.
The reality of my situation may not change;
    but the agony I am experiencing can be reduced
    and the healing balm of releasing my pain
      can restore me.
I bring my pain, my rawness with me today
    as I allow myself to name the pains so I can release them.

MEDITATION B
[Walk to the Minnehaha Pavilion.]

As I gently set my intention of embracing my pain,
    I do not allow myself to be overwhelmed
      by its force or retreat from its fury.
I seek awareness of the power, energy, and truth
    of the pain I carry.

Pain is the opening of my heart only to have it crushed.
It's the utter emptiness of knowing that the loss experienced
    feels completely overwhelming, unfair, and undeniable.

I feel so powerless.....every part of me hurts.
Getting up, walking, eating, even breathing hurts
        because of my pain.

MEDITATION C
[Walk to the bridge over the Falls.]

As I stand at the Falls and watch the Minnehaha Creek cascade,
        the waters are symbolic of my pain:
           pain beyond control...beyond containment.
"My God, my God, why have You abandoned me?
Why are You so far from me?
O my God, I cry by day, but you do not answer
        and by night, I find no rest."[5]

This pain is a deep and permeating black hole of emptiness.
I have tried and tried and tried and I am spent.
I have nothing left to give.
I don't know what to do or where to move or how to be anymore.
Pain and desolation suck me dry.
I have no hope.

MEDITATION D
[Walk to steps on the north side of Falls.]

As I walk to the steps, I hold my paper with all my pain listed.
This list is mine: mine to hold, mine to release.
As I walk down the steps, with each step,
        conscious of my physical safety on the steps,
        I name each suffering.

[Walk down the first 23 steps.
Sit at the bench; reflect on the weight and depth of the pain.
Walk down the next 40 steps. Sit on the bench.
Put two to three sunflower seeds in the mouth,
        but do not break them.]

---

5   Psalm 22: 1-3

I taste the salt.
As it lingers in my mouth,
       the salt reminds me of the bitterness of my pain.

[Without opening the seeds, spit them into the garbage bag
       and continue down to the bottom.

Walk along the north side of Minnehaha Creek
Listen to the pounding of the water.

MEDITATION E
Consider the weight and depth of your pain.]

I am at the bottom, physically, emotionally, spiritually.
It's been a hard, difficult journey and I am empty.
As I walk the path on this side of the falls,
       I know I need to make some changes.
I can't go on like this...the pain is too much for me.
I need help.
I need to let go.
I need hope.
I need.

As I stand, full of pain, in this beautiful environment,
       I breathe in "openness"
          so that I may find what I need to be healed.

MEDITATION F
[Move to the middle of the bridge crossing the Creek.]

I stand in the middle of the bridge over Minnehaha Creek
       seeking a way to release my pain,
       searching for meaning that has vanished.

"Your pain is the breaking of the shell
       that encloses your understanding."[6]

---

6   Kahlil Gibran, http://www.katsandogz.com/onpain.html (April 19, 2016).

As I take two or three sunflower seeds in my mouth,
        again I taste the salt, the bitterness of my pain.
But it is time to break open the shell to find what I need:
        the morsel of understanding,
        the seed of courage, the spark of hope.

[Break open the sunflower seeds, eat the seeds inside,
        put the shells in the garbage bag.]

Spirit of the Universe,
I have tasted the salt and it has lingered in my mouth too long.
This defensive shell I built around me for protection was once
        a useful shield but now it's an isolating barrier
        keeping me from myself and from others.

May my pain be tasted and then washed away
        like the salt in my mouth.
May I break open the shell of isolation and despair
        in order to find the seeds of healing.
May I discover the lessons and gifts hidden within my suffering
        trusting that not only are they there
        but they will be nourishment for my healing.

MEDITATION G
[Cross the bridge to south side of the Creek.
        on the rocks at the edge of the Creek.
Take out the paper of pains and re-read them.]

I choose to release my pain to the Earth.
I have carried it long enough and it is time to let it go.
May the rejuvenating power of the Earth
        transform my pain into new life.
May the Spirit of all creation grant me a renewed spirit
        empowered by the greater understanding
        and deeper wisdom of my pain.

[Eat more seeds mindful of the analogy of breaking open shells.]

MEDITATION H
[Tear the page of pains into small pieces.
Hold the pieces or put them in a pocket.
Begin climbing, stopping at the landing
      of the 49th step after third set of stairs.
Eat more seeds on the way up.]

"Even though you may want to move forward in your life
      you may have one foot on the brakes.
In order to be free, we must learn how to let go.

Release the hurt; release the fear.
Refuse to entertain your old pain.

The energy it takes to hang onto the past is holding you
      back from a new life.
What is it you would let go of today?"[7]

I am afraid to let go completely.
      What will happen if I do?
Does it mean I didn't really love what I lost?
      Does it mean I will forget?
As I touch the torn pieces of paper
      I trust the process of letting go.

Letting go does not mean I didn't love completely.
It does not mean I am letting go of the memories
      or the blessings received.
Letting go means I release the isolation and desperation;
      I don't have to be alone any more.

Letting go means the pain is not dominating me anymore.
It means I trust that in turning over my pain to Earth and Divinity,
      I am entrusting it to a Power greater than myself.
Letting go means I can welcome joy into my life again,
      without guilt or regret.
It means I can kindle the spark of hope into a flame of liberation.

---

[7] Mary Manin Morrissey, http://www.brainyquote.com/quotes/quotes/m/mary-maninm524141.html/' (April 19, 2016).

MEDITATION I
[Climb to top; walk to the bridge over the Falls.]

As I stand at the Falls and watch the Minnehaha Creek cascade,
    the waters are symbolic of releasing my pain,
        inviting it to flow over the Falls, down the Creek,
            into the Mississippi River,
        out to the Gulf of Mexico, and into the Atlantic Ocean.

May the waters, signify my movement
    guided by the Unseen Current of Earth and Divinity
    to a place where my heart is once again open
    and my spirit is free.

I choose to release the pieces of paper
    into my garbage bag with the empty shells.
If today, I can release all the pieces, great.
If today, I can release half the pieces, great.
If today, I can only release a few pieces, great.
I accept what I can do today with gratitude.

[Walk to a recycling bin, and release your bag of garbage.]

Just as this organic refuse is recycled
    my pain has been transformed.
I go forth in thanksgiving for
    the empowering courage that I faced my pain
        and it did not defeat me,
    the deeper understanding that my pain has birthed in me.
    and the reassuring hope that the Unseen Current
        of Earth and Divinity walks with me.

So be it. Amen.

4.
THE WAY
OF
RE-MEMBERING GOD

Stella Maris Chapel
St. John's Abby & University
Collegeville, MN

LOCATION	St. John's Abby & University, Collegeville, MN
BRING	Drinking water, insect repellant
LENGTH	3 miles
TIME	2 hours

MEDITATION A
[Arrive at St. John's Parking lot in front of Abby church.]

Fear is the greatest motivating force on this planet.
We are afraid of everything from asteroids to zombies
    and everyone from addicts to zealots.
Often we hope to hide the fear under the volume
    and dazzle of avoidance techniques.
We disguise our fear by accumulating stuff,
    escaping into addictions or relationships,
    cowering in a world we think
        is only dangerous and deadly.
Because we are so often unconscious of the fear, it controls us.
We live afraid.

MEDITATION B
[Walk to the beach at Lake Sagatagan.
Consider how fear motivates me.
Stop at the beach of Lake Sagatagan.]

No matter how we attempt to dismiss it,
    the reality is our fear remains.
And when we finally embark on the great adventure
    to uncover the source of our fear,
    we are shocked by the discovery.
The primal fear of all humanity is that God has abandoned us.[8]

---

[8] Roger Bernstrom, conversation with author, (Minneapolis, MN, September 8, 2015).

MEDITATION C
[Take the trail east, to the left of the beach.
Keeping to the trail closest to the lake,
walk to the statue of St. Kateri Tekawitha.]
I fear I am different from the Divine.
Because I have a physical body,
    I think this separates me from God.
How can God relate to me with my weight issues,
    alcohol addiction, desire to play video games,
    passion for mystery novels, love of dancing,
    fits of anger, and uncontrollable sobbing?

The Divine doesn't do any of that stuff.
This is the domain of the human condition,
    this realm of bodies, that function marvelously
        and eventually break down,
    this realm of emotions,
        that swing from utter joy to utter despair,
    this realm of thinking, that indulges thoughts
        that I am enough without the Divine..
How can God relate to that?

MEDITATION D
[Walk to where the trail turns right to the south.]

I fear because I am guilty.
I have committed grievous offenses against others and myself.
I have hated others with zest, stolen items without remorse,
    gossiped greedily, indulged in self-righteous egotism
    without concern for others' reputations or feelings.
I have refused forgiveness and refused to forgive.
I have denied and circumvented Truth.
I have turned away from Love.
I have run away from the Divine.
The guilt weighs so heavily upon me,
    I can see no way to unburden myself.

MEDITATION E
[Walk to the first wooden bridge.]

I fear I am unworthy to be loved.
I am so unimportant, so inconsequential.
Sometimes I try to hide behind attitude, others,
    or stuff to show the world I am special.
But I don't feel special.
I am not the best at anything, have no great talent,
    can't lead the world to peace.
In my commonness,
    I don't bring anything valuable to my circumstance.

On the outside I look ordinary; on the inside I feel vacant.
I am insignificant, empty.
I feel unloved, unlovable.
I am worthless.

MEDITATION F
[Walk for ten minutes.]

I fear because I am broken.
Shame permeates my being.
I have been split apart, broken into a million pieces,
    damaged beyond repair.
Others have wounded me; I have wounded others.
The results are always the same.
Whether victim or perpetrator,
    I am a fractured human being.
There is no way I can be put back together, re-built, repaired, made whole.
I am damaged goods.

MEDITATION G
[Walk for ten minutes.]

I feel unconnected.
Everyone else seems to have what they need and want.
I miss the love of family, the comfort of friends.

I long for relationships filled with warmth, laughter, tenderness.
    depth, integrity, sweetness, and wonder.
I feel like I am trying, praying, pleading but the answer is 'no".
Sensing a wasted life, I am lost.
On some level, I know that this is not true
    but that's how it feels today.
I feel left out, unconnected.

MEDITATION H
[Walk to the second wooden bridge.].

I fear I am alone.
I don't feel You or Your Presence.
Nothing is going my way and life is so hard.
Pain fills me to overflowing:
    pain from death, lost friendships, empty promises,
      broken dreams, vanished hope.
There is no balm for my ache, no comfort for my agony.
Spiritual leaders say You are here
    but I don't feel You or sense You at all.
I just know I feel all alone, abandoned, deserted.
Where are You?
I don't know.

MEDITATION I
[Walk to Stella Maris Chapel.

Everything we do is rooted in this fear
    that we are unconnected to the Source of all creation.
We try to climb the ladder of "success",
    stepping on others and the planet to get to the top,
    under the fallacy that then we will be "God"
    and not feel this agonizing separation.
We cling to others in hopes that they will fill us up.
We buy and buy and buy, insulating our spaces
    with stuff to feel the comfort of acquisitions.

But nothing fills our need; nothing calms this fear
    that we are different, guilty, unworthy,
      broken, unconnected, alone.

Nothing but the truth.
And the truth is: we <u>are</u> connected.
We are in fact <u>One</u> with the Divine.
And always have been.
And always will be.

[Enjoy the beauty of Stella Maris Chapel and Lake Sagatagan.]

MEDITATION J
[Head back to St. John's Abbey
    stopping at the first wooden bridge.]

Though I look different from the Divine,
    we are the same.
Though I am not the totality of the One,
    we share the same power, spirit, beauty, strength
    wisdom, insight, truth, timelessness.

CELEBRATION OF UNITY
The same Power that commands the sun to rise is within me.
The same Serenity of the golden sun setting is within me.

The same Radiance of sunlight shimmering through the pines
dances through me.
The same Wonder of a seed, broken open searching for Light,
dances through me.
The same Beauty of an opening yellow rose dances through me.

The same Majesty of the snow-capped Rocky Mountains
is my Majesty.
The same Illumination of a lightning strike is my Illumination.
The same Strength of a raging tornado wind is my Strength.

The Depth of the Pacific Ocean is the same Depth of my soul.
The Reach of the furthest galaxy is the same Reach of my soul.

MEDITATION K
[Walk for ten minutes.]

I am guilty and forgiven.
Of course I have hurt myself and others.
I am human.

Having taken this body, heart, mind, and soul,
    I have and will make errors,
        sometimes devastating ones.

THE POWER OF FORGIVENESS
There is no transgression that lies beyond Divine mercy.
All sins forgivable.
There is no point in existence where I am a better sinner than God is a forgiver.
All sins forgivable.
The Divine is Complete Clemency, Total Acceptance.
If I am far from the Divine, it is I who have moved.

The one I struggle to forgive is me.
I leave the harsh judgement, strict punishments in the waters
to be transformed into understanding and compassion.

As I admit my mistakes, faults, and defects as uniquely mine,
I accept responsibility for all of them.
As I responsibly make apologies,
I accept my role in all situations.
As I make amends, I seek to heal what I have wounded.
All sins forgivable.
All I need do is ask.

MEDITATION L
[Walk for ten minutes.]

Though I feel unworthy, I <u>am</u> worthy.
I have chosen this life, it is uniquely mine.
Because I am, I have significance.
I am loved, and lovable—indeed, worthy.

WORTHY

If I am unlovable, then God is not Love.
If I am unworthy, then God is undesirable.
Impossible—that the Lover is not Love!
Inconceivable—that the Compassionate One is not desired!

Everything is significant
because all creation shares the essence of the Source of Being.
There is no such thing as unworthy
because all creation dances in the rhythm of the Source of Life.
And the Source is very significant, very worthy.
And that makes me so as well.

MEDITATION M
[Walk to the second wooden bridge.]

I am broken and yet whole.
Yes I have many severe wounds but they are in my life,
    not to thwart my movement
    but to enhance my understanding.
Every wound has a lesson,
    ultimately guiding me back to the reality of my wholeness
    and to the comprehension that
    I am always partnered to the Whole.

STILL

If I lose my sight, I will still see your Beauty.
If I lose my hearing, I will still hear your Voice.

If I lose my trust in humankind, I will still hope in your Truth.
If I lose the love of my life, I will still embrace your Love.

If I lose my fingers, I will still touch your Presence.
If I lose my ability to be employed, I will still work to do your Will.

If I lose faith in myself, I will cling to your Faith.
If I am defeated by life, I will surrender to your Side.

If I lose my mobility, I will still follow your Way.
If I lose my mind, I will still comprehend your Presence.

If I lose my way, I will still chart your Path.
If I lose my life, I will still be One with You.

MEDITATION N
[Walk to where the trail turns left to the west.]

I am connected.
Even when I do not feel a part of anything,
    I am always part of all creation, part of the Whole.

FULFILLMENT
Without the rose, the garden is merely flowers.
Without music, the notes would be just noise.
Without color, the sunset would be dull.

There is nothing common about
the sunflower turning toward the Light.
There is nothing ordinary about the rose opening to Life.

How less the world would be
if the only breed of dog was Chihuahua.
How empty the forest would look without trees of pine.

The least significant bug teems with purpose.
Every part of this planet is alive,
alive with purpose,
alive with interconnectedness,
alive with interdependency.

Without you, your tasks go unfulfilled.
Without you, the earth will be more wounded.
Without you, the world is empty.

You are essential to the Whole.
You are indispensable.

MEDITATION O
[Walk to the statue of St. Kateri Tekawitha.]

Though I feel alone, You are with me.
No matter what happens, You are with me and I am with You.

> YOU AND I ARE ONE.
> We are dancing when my heart soars in joy.
> We are in silent reflection as I gaze over the lake.
>
> We are in my tears when I feel abandoned.
> We are in my fury when my anger explodes.
>
> You and I are One.
> You are always with me for how can I escape myself?

MEDITATION P
[Walk to the beach.]

The truth is we are always in the Presence
    because we are part of the Presence
Nothing can exist apart from God;
    therefore nothing can be apart from God.
Re-membering means our original state is membered to God
    and our task is to re-member that reality.[9]
We are part of the Whole.
We are One.

> BEFORE
> In the beginning before matter and spirit separated,
> there was Presence.
> Before body and soul became competitors,
> there was Unity.
> Before the Sun and Moon commanded day and night,
> there was Timelessness.
>
> In the beginning before masculine and feminine divorced,
> there was Love.
>
> Before the dualism of the physical and the spiritual,
> there was Solidarity.
> Before the hierarchy of two-leggeds over four-leggeds,
> there was Alliance.

---

[9] Elizabeth Caldwell, Leaving Home With Faith, (Cleveland: Pilgrim Press, 2000), 16.

Before there was right and wrong, left and right,
there was Harmony.
Before there was winning and losing,
there was Wonder.
Before there was science and religion,
there was Mystery.

In the beginning before idolatry led to trickery,
there was Truth.
Before anxiety led to violence,
there was Peace.
Before the fear led to separation,
there was One.

5.
THE WAY
OF
HEALING WOUNDS

Fort Snelling State Park
Mississippi & Minnesota Rivers
St. Paul MN

LOCATION	Parking lot at Gift Shop, Fort Snelling State Park
BRING	Drinking water, insect repellant,

                     a fearless and moral inventory of myself
                            paying particular attention to issues of
                            egotism, dishonesty, sexual misconduct,
                            resentments, bullying, greed, addictions,
                            self-righteousness, arrogance, hatred.

LENGTH	7 miles
TIME	3 hours

MEDITATION A
[Arrive at parking lot at northwest corner of Snelling Lake
    at Fort Snelling State Park]

Healing wounds begins with the activity of reviewing my actions
    taking inventory of my attitudes and behaviors
    where I have wounded myself and others
    and feeling contrition or regret for past wrongs.
It involves a commitment to personal change
    and the resolve to live a life of greater integrity,
responsibility, and compassion.
Today I am looking at myself reviewing
    my personal patterns of thought and action,
    my communal behaviors, and my global attitudes.

"The heavens will not be filled with those
    who never made mistakes
    but with those who recognized that they were off course
    and who corrected their ways
      to get back in the light of truth."[10]

---

10   Dieter F. Uchtdorf, http://www.goodreads.com/quotes/tag/repentance (September 23, 2015).

MEDITATION B
[Begin walking east, left as you face the lake.
Walk to the beach of Lake Snelling.]

"Take a walk through the garden of forgiveness
        and pick a flower of forgiveness for everything
           you have ever done."[11]

I seek to make amends for my attitudes and behaviors
        that hurt myself.
I forgive myself for the times I let fear dominate me:
        when I acted with callous disregard
        for my health or the health of others
        and when I refused to act because I was afraid
I forgive myself for the times I wallowed in self-pity:
        playing the victim,
        expecting others to save me rather than act for myself.

I forgive myself for the times I strutted in egotism:
        thinking and acting as if I was the most important person,
        as if my answers were the only answers for all.

I forgive myself for the times I allowed self-hatred:
        when I consciously and unconsciously hurt myself
        because I believed I deserved it.

I make amends to myself by inviting
        the waters of forgiveness to wash me clean
        and carry me to the shores of reconciliation.

---

[11]   Steven Richards, https://apps.hclib.org/account/items/index.cfm (February 8, 2016).

MEDITATION C
[Continue walking east. Cross the road.
Walk to the entrance station of the park.]

"Death is in the power of the tongue."[12]
I seek forgiveness for all the times
    I used hate filled and savage words
    on my family, friends, fellow employees and employers,
    stores, businesses, and offices I patronize.

I seek forgiveness for all the times I cheated another:
    when I stole and justified it
    when I refused to do my fair share
        out of a sense of entitlement

I seek forgiveness for all the times
    I allowed resentment to dictate:
    when I said poisoned words to express my feelings
    when I was passive aggressive and pouted
    when I was just plain aggressive and cruel.

I seek forgiveness for all the times
    I failed to express my emotions in a healthy way:
    using anger as a weapon to hurt others
        falsely thinking hurting someone else
        would heal my own pain
    using guilt or shame to manipulate others in
        to doing what I desire
    using blame to judge and condemn.

I seek forgiveness and the path of that forgiveness is
    admitting, apologizing, and amending.
Today I do the admitting.
Then I must do the apologizing and amending to each person.
I seek forgiveness from others.
If one does not accept my apology, that is his/her right.
My job is to admit take responsibility for my shortcomings
    in order to be released from the weight of my wrongs.

I am willing to make amends to them all.
May the waters of forgiveness wash me clean
    and carry me to the shores of reconciliation.

---

[12]   Proverbs 18: 21.

MEDITATION D
[Walk to the Visitor's Center/Gift Shop.
Enter and read the Native history of this site.
Then go to the Dakota Memorial.]

"It's a universal law—
      intolerance is the first sign of an inadequate education.
An ill-educated person behaves with arrogant impatience
      whereas truly profound education breeds humility."[13]

I seek forgiveness for any attitudes and actions of prejudice
      times I believed my ethnicity was better than others
      times I looked down on others who were not my color
      times I believed stereotypes in order to feel superior.

As a white American I seek forgiveness
      that our bigotry has generated such toxicity
        into the fabric of America for centuries.
I seek forgiveness for all Americans who promoted
      white supremacy in any form.
I seek forgiveness for all Americans who led first
      with building walls rather than building bridges.
I seek forgiveness for all Americans who resorted to
      bullying, persecution, and torture
      to dominate and control another human being.
I seek forgiveness for all Americans who believed
      that killing people of color meant white security.

I am willing to make amends
      by cultivating an attitude of tolerance and acceptance.
I commit to teaching by example that all humanity
      regardless of color, ethnicity, heritage, or homeland
      is worthy of dignity and respect.
There is only one race—the human race.
      We are They.
      They are Us.

May the waters of forgiveness wash me clean
      and carry me to the shores of reconciliation.

---

13   Aleksandr Solzhenitsyn, http://www.goodreads.com/quotes/tag/tolerance (February 8, 2016).

MEDITATION E
Walk to Pike Island.
Walk to the confluence of the MN and MS Rivers.]

"God has a thousand names, or rather, God is nameless....
In my opinion, Rama, God, Yahweh, or Allah are all attempts
    on the part of humanity to name that invisible force....
We can only conceive of God
    within the limitations of our own minds.
What matters then, whether
    one man worships as a person and another as a force?
Both do right according to their lights.
One need only remember that God is the force among the forces.
All other forces are material.

God is the vital force or spirit,
    which is all-pervading, all embracing,
      and therefore beyond human ken."[14]

All religions have been persecuted and persecuted others
    in the name of God.
I seek forgiveness for all the hurt and pain caused
    by using religion as a weapon.

As one raised Catholic Christian,
    I seek forgiveness for Christians guilty of sexual abuse.
I seek forgiveness for Christians guilty of covering up sexual abuse
    in order to maintain their status of power and prestige.
I seek forgiveness for Christians guilty of spiritual abuse
    using the fear of damnation or separation from the Divine
as a means of conversion.
I seek forgiveness for Christians who
    belong to white supremacists groups
    advocating God and country at any cost.
I seek forgiveness for Christians who bomb abortion clinics
    erroneously believing that killing people to stop abortions
is a justifiable moral stand.

---

[14]   Mohandas Gandhi, The Path to God, Berkeley, CA: Berkeley Hills Books, 19999), 38-39.

I seek forgiveness for Christians who believe and promote
        that their religion is the only path to God,
          judging and condemning others
              who follow a different way.

The One we all seek asks that we love tenderly without exception
        act justly without malice or superiority
        walk humbly whichever path is ours.[15]

May the waters of forgiveness wash me clean
        and carry me to the shores of reconciliation.

MEDITATION F
[At the confluence of the MN and MS Rivers]

"The wound is the place where the Light enters you."[16]

I seek to heal all wounds—
        personal, family, communal, national, and global.
No more denial
        pretending that my attitudes and actions
            have not inflicted great suffering,
        fantasizing we are blameless rather than responsible
        acquiescing by silence
            my power to change the outcome.
No more hiding behind accomplishments that don't erase
        the shame, hatred, cruelty, violence, and immorality
inflicted on others
It merely covers the action with a veneer of pride and ego.

No more silent apologies
        that keep the action hidden from public view
        that keep me from being rigorously honest
        that maintains the prideful image of my perfectionism.

---

15   Based on Micah 6: 8.
16   Rumi, http://www.goodreads.com/quotes/tag/healing (February 8, 2016).

No more failure to make amends
        out of fear of being unforgiven or rejected
        out of fear of being seen as I really am—
            a fractured human being.

I commit to the path to healing wounds by:
        taking a fearless and moral inventory of myself
          making authentic apologies, honest amends,
              and holistic repentance.
That is the path of dignity restored.

MEDITATION G
[Walk back to the parking lot at northwest corner of Snelling Lake. Enjoy the Beauty, the Sacred, the Oneness.]

"Nothing erases the past.
There is repentance
      there is atonement
      and there is forgiveness.
That is all, but that is enough."[17]

---

17   Ted Chiang, http://www.goodreads.com/quotes/tag/repentance , (September 23, 2015).

6.

THE WAY OF RECOVERING SANITY

Lake Phalen
St. Paul, MN

LOCATION   Lake Phalen, St. Paul
BRING   Drinking water
LENGTH   3 miles
TIME   2 hours

This ritual is based on
    the Twelve Steps of Alcoholics Anonymous.[18]
You do not need to be an addict to utilize the benefits
    of these simple and profound steps.
They are a foundation for all who seek to recover sanity
    and deepen spiritual health.

MEDITATION A
[Arrive the parking lot, north end of Lake Phalen.]

ADMITTED POWERLESSNESS
May I take the first step with abandon.
I am powerless over so much:
    the future and the past,
    the opinions and behaviors of others,
        despite all my efforts to control them,
    my own compulsive and negative thinking,
        which often lead to unhealthy actions.

Today I stand powerless over the things, people,
    and my own self-destructive attitudes.
I admit I am powerless and my unhealthy obsessions
    make my life unmanageable

---

[18] Twelve Steps and Twelve Traditions, (New York City, NY: Alcoholics Anonymous Worldwide Services, 1952), 5-9.

MEDITATION B
[Begin walking east toward the left as you face the lake
    stopping along the north-eastern shore.]

CAME TO BELIEVE
May I take the second step with faith.
I have tried for so long to be in control and not need anyone else.
Caught between my pride—
    not wanting to admit vulnerability or weakness—
    and my despair—
    feeling I was unworthy of being helped or saved—
    I wallowed alone in fear.
Today I have come to believe a power greater than myself
    can and will restore my sanity.
I believe.

MEDITATION C
[Walk ¼ of the eastern shore.]

TURN MY WILL OVER
May I take the third step with trust.
This is a scary step of surrender
    rooted in powerlessness and faith.
I wrestle with control and now give it up
    all my attempts to manipulate things my way
    all my efforts where my ego is in charge
    all my false beliefs that I know best. .
I yield to Your care, trusting that You will grant me all I need.
Today I make the decision to turn my will and my life
    over to the care of the Source of Life.

MEDITATION D
[Walk ½ of the eastern shore.]

INVENTORY
May I take the fourth step with clarity.
Where has my conscience been tugging at me
    and where have I refused to listen?
What character defects interfere with my authenticity?
    With my integrity?
Where am I hiding in denial?
May I take a fearless and moral inventory of myself,
    being rigorously honest about
    my strengths and weakness.

MEDITATION E
[Walk ¾ of the eastern shore.]

ADMITTED
May I take the fifth step courageously.
Confession is a beneficial necessity that brings reality to light.
    and lances open the wounds I have inflicted
        so they may be healed.
I need to state my faults and defects out loud
    to myself, to the Divine, and to another person
        despite embarrassment and shame.
This is the only path to decreasing the ache of being imperfect
    and cleansing the infections my defects have caused.

Today I admit to myself
    and to my Higher Power the exact nature of my wrongs
        and I commit to admitting them to another human being.

MEDITATION F
[Walk along the south shore.]

ENTIRELY READY
May I take the sixth step with earnestness.
There are times when I am ready to give up my defects
    but then something happens—
    temptation sneaks in, fear captures me—
    and I pick up my defects like old friends.
They don't help me live a life of recovery
    but I choose to indulge in them anyway.
Today, I am entirely ready to have the Source
    remove my shortcomings
And I am entirely ready to have the Source keep them.

MEDITATION G
[Walk along the south shore.].

HUMBLY ASKED
May I take the seventh step with humility.
Because I am powerless over my defects
 I let go of my pride and ask for Divine assistance.
I can only walk a path of integrity
 with aid from a Power greater than myself.

My job is to continually invite that Higher Power in,
 listen, and let go of my own will
 in order to do the will of God.
I humbly ask God to remove all my shortcomings
 and every single thing in my life
 that separates me from the Divine.

MEDITATION H
[Walk to the beach on the south-west corner.]

BECAME READY
May I take the eighth step with confidence
I have made many mistakes that harmed others:
 some consciously , some unconsciously
 some covertly, some overtly.
Now I search my heart and memory for all the persons I harmed.
 To whom have I lied?
 To whom have I cheated?
 To whom have I been violent:
 physically, emotionally, mentally, spiritually?
 Whom have I hated?
 Whom have I refused to love?

I make my list today of all persons I have harmed
 and I resolve to adding names to my list
 as my conscience dictates.
I am ready to make amends to them all.

MEDITATION I
[Walk to the Lake Phalen Activity Club.]

MAKE AMENDS
May I take the ninth step with fearlessness.
It is not enough to admit my errors.
I need to make amends for all the harm I have caused.

This begins with a direct apology
        and ends with repaying, rebuilding, and fixing
        what I have broken.

I do this step regardless of my fear or pride or shame
        except when to do so would cause further harm.

At this time,
        in this place,
        I promise to make direct amends to all I have harmed.

MEDITATION J
Walk to the picnic area.]

CONTINUED
May I take the tenth step with tenacity.
It is so easy to fall back into old habits.
A daily self-reflective review shows me where
        I have forgotten I was powerless
                and tried to manage my life on my own,
        I forgot my Higher Power,
        I tried to exert my will, my ego, my control,
        I resorted to character defects
                that hurt myself and others,
        I refused to listen to the Source of Life.

I cannot afford to neglect my spiritual health for even one day.
Each and every day, I continue to take my own personal inventory
        and when I am wrong, I promptly admit it.

MEDITATION K
[Walk to the water falls.]

IMPROVE CONSCIOUS CONTACT
May I take the eleventh step with gratitude.
The Divine and I are in a relationship, a partnership.
This means I have a responsibility
    to listen and speak,
    to question and answer.

I seek through whatever means I choose
    —prayer, meditation, nature—
    to improve my conscious contact with the Divine.
I pray only for the knowledge of Divine Will
    and the power to carry it out.

MEDITATION L
Walk back to parking lot.]

PRACTICE THESE PRINCIPLES
I take the twelfth step with conviction.
When I was addicted, I did what I wanted.
When I entered sobriety,
    I did what I needed to do to be in recovery.
As I sought conscious contact with the Divine,
    I chose to be in partnership
        with the God of my understanding.
As I surrender, I allow the Spirit of the Universe to lead me.
Now I find myself full circle:
    what I want is for God to lead me and for me to follow.

My integrity and recovery are the most important foundations
    of my life.
Having had a spiritual awakening as a result of these twelve steps,
    I pledge to practice these principles in all my affairs
    and carry the message of these steps to all others.

7.
THE WAY
OF
UNDERSTANDING ONE

Lake Harriet
Minneapolis, MN

LOCATION	Lake Harriet, Minneapolis
BRING	Drinking water
LENGTH	3 miles
TIME	2 hours

MEDITATION A
[Arrive and park.]

Who is this being we call God?
There are countless names:
    God, the Divine, Allah, Supreme Being, Higher Power.
Through our efforts, we seek to understand
    the breadth and depth of the Divine.

Whatever words we use, our vocabulary fails
    to fully identify this Entity.
The ancient writer of Exodus quotes God naming God's self as I AM.
I AM is a title without equal
    for it speaks of identity without labels
    of essence without limits.
The great I AM is undefinable, yet present.

This indefinability is difficult for us humans.
We want a God we can relate to, who is like us.
So we make God human:
    a father, a friend, a rescuer, a lover
Though they provide partial identity to the Divine, we seek more.

As we seek to understand
    this abstract and immaterial concept of I AM,
    we explore four less common,
    non-anthropomorphic descriptions.
I AM is Truth, Consciousness, Mystery, Presence.

MEDITATION B
[Begin walking south, left as I face Lake Harriet
        stopping approximately halfway between
        the north and south ends of the lake]
I AM is Truth.

VOICES
Why is it we so easily listen to the voice of falsehood
yet find it so hard to hear the voice of Truth?

When we hear the voice of ego we believe it without question.
When we hear the Voice of the One we question our sanity.

We gravitate to the voice of temptation,
ignoring the voice of Reality.
We run to the voice of fear, shutting out the voice of Hope.

The Voice of Truth is a soft whisper deep within the heart
ever resolute and stubbornly persistent
regardless of our barriers or rejections.

Because I AM is the certainty of Truth
the Voice of Truth needs no defense from attack,
 no explanation for clarity
no justification for being.
Truth simply is.

Open my heart, O Truth.
Help me to hear, listen, and embrace Truth
as You reveal Yourself to me today.

MEDITATION C
[Continue walking, stopping approximately halfway
        between the east and west sides of the lake.]

I AM is Consciousness

STATE OF BEING

Unconscious, I am alive but not living
taking in air, but not breathing
Consciousness is being alive, present in the moment
breathing in and breathing out
the oxygen of awareness.
Unconsciousness is being preoccupied with thoughts,
but not discerning
sometimes spinning in the befuddlement of inaction
other times spinning in the chaos of busyness.

Consciousness plucks me from the abyss of obsession
back to the solid ground of knowing
grounded not in discombobulation
but in awareness.
Unconsciousness is being lost;
consciousness is being my authentic self.

Open my heart, O Consciousness.
Help me to face, enjoy and walk in Consciousness
as You reveal Yourself to me today.

MEDITATION D
[Continue walking, stopping approximately halfway
between the south and north sides of the lake.]

I AM is Mystery

MYSTERY
The Divine: Horizon, seen yet untouchable.
The Source: Darkness from which all things have their being
The Beginning: Light from which all things are sustained.

The Indescribable: unnamable yet recognizable.
The Enigmatic: unexplainable yet experienced.

The Earth: deep and penetrating restorative energy.
The Sky: broad and expansive illuminating energy.

Incomprehensible: atom and galaxy.
Mystery: Within and Beyond.

MEDITATION E
Continue walking, stopping approximately halfway
 between the west and east sides of the lake.]

I AM is Presence.

I AM
There is an Energy that connects all creation
 flowing through and within all that exists.
I AM that energy, that force.

When you are lonely, I AM the soft whispers of hope.
When you are lost, I AM the light breaking through the fog.
When you are weeping, I AM the tender cloth that holds your tears.

When you are joyful, I AM the radiance bursting from your face.
When you overcome great difficulties,
I AM the sweet rapture of satisfaction.

When you are successful, I AM the head cheerleader.
When you are hurt, I AM the first responder.

I am Presence
with you, within you.

MEDITATION F
[Walk to the Rose Garden.]

I see You everywhere
 in the roses, their colors and scents
 on the water, whether calm and placid or wild and roaring
 in the trees that reach up and grow down to You
 within my fellow travelers on this journey.

I see You everywhere
You are everywhere
You are everything
You Are

8.

*THE WAY
OF
KINDLING JOY*

Yellow & Purple Iris

LOCATION	Walker's choice
BRING	Drinking water
LENGTH	2 miles
TIME	1 hour

Red Rose

MEDITATION A
Arrive and park.]
Joy is a decision - - a choice.
I pledge to break out of my prison of my own building
        my prison of fear and anxiety and worry and control
        and today I choose joy.

I constructed the walls to keep others out
        but in reality I have only kept myself in.
In trying to control everything
        I have only managed to waste valuable time
        in a futile effort.
Today I tear down my prison walls and breathe in the joy of
        spontaneity, creativity, daring, bliss, ingenuity, authenticity.

Yes, there will be trials but joy will not let me down.
Yes, there will be disappointments but joy will sustain me.

Joy is a decision - - a choice.
I pledge to break out of my prison of my own building
        my prison of fear and anxiety
        and today I choose joy.

Orange Roses

MEDITATION B
[Begin.
Walk slowly for 10-12 minutes]
Joy is trust.
I pledge to trust that all events are unfolding as they should.

This is a beautiful and harsh place, this earth we live on.
Our lives, too, are beautiful and harsh.

Today I trust that there is a Source of Life
      beyond my understanding.
Today because I trust the Source of Life
      I know and trust that all life is unfolding as it should.

I trust that beyond the violence lay acceptance
      beyond the bleakness lay hope.
I trust that beyond the guilt lay forgiveness
      beyond the pain lay healing.
I trust that beyond the brokenness lay wholeness.

Today I pledge to trust

Iris in the Rushes

MEDITATION C
[Walk slowly for 10-12 minutes]
Joy is wonder.
I pledge to notice the total reality around me.

May I enjoy the rose petals rather than complain about the thorns
     embrace the fragrance rather than the fertilizer.

May I understand that life is about lessons
     not punishments or rewards.
May I look beyond the surface of the calamity
     to find the small miracles hidden
          in the breadth and depth of life.

Joy is wonder.
I pledge to notice the total reality around me.

Blue Pansies

MEDITATION D
[Walk slowly for 10-12 minutes]
Joy is curiosity.
I pledge to be inquisitive about all the lessons of my life.

TEACH ME[19]
When You don't move the mountains, teach me to climb.
When You don't part the waters, teach me to swim.

When You don't create an oasis, teach me to search.
When You don't provide manna, teach me to plant.

When You don't stop the lightening, teach me to be grounded.
When you don't shift the wind, teach me to ride the current.

When You don't eliminate the hurdle, teach me to hope.
When You don't remove my enemy, teach me to love.

When You don't feel present, teach me to trust.
When You ask me to step off the cliff with no safety net,
    teach me to fly.

Joy is curiosity.
I pledge to be inquisitive about all the lessons of my life.

---

19   Inspired by Trust In Me, by Lauren Daigle.

White Crocus

MEDITATION E

[Walk slowly for 10-12 minutes]
Joy is gratitude.
I pledge to fill my heart with gratitude and thanksgiving.

For all my lessons, I am grateful.
For all who loved me and refused to love me, I am grateful.
For the ache in my heart when I suffered loss, I am grateful.
For the excitement of success, I am grateful.

Joy is gratitude.
I pledge to fill my heart with gratitude and thanksgiving.

Purple Lilacs

MEDITATION F
[Walk to parking space.]
Joy is the surrender.
I pledge to turn my will and my life over to the care of the One.

I am / I AM[20]
I am running to I AM after spending years running away.
I am seeking I AM because I am powerless on my own.
I am wishing I AM to be my Guide
even when I think I know where I am going.
I am breathing in I AM
I am IAM.

---

20   Inspired by Running by Gateway Worship.

White Calla Lily

www.ingramcontent.com/pod-product-compliance
Lightning Source LLC
Chambersburg PA
CBHW040330300426
44113CB00020B/2707